Situated in the north-east corner of East Anglia, the Norfolk Broads harbour some of the richest wetlands left in Britain; they are certainly among the most extensive. The Broads proper are the wide channels of water that so characterise the region. For the purposes of this book, however, all the other wetland habitats associated with the Norfolk Broads are also included and the proximity of the North Sea cannot be ignored.

The range of habitats found in the Norfolk Broads covers most freshwater and wetland ecosystems that could be expected to occur in lowland Britain as a whole. In addition to rivers and Broads, there are ponds, lakes, dikes and ditches, while on the land-based fringes there are marshes, fens, bogs, carr woodlands and grazing meadows.

With all this diversity in habitat, it is not surprising that the range of wildlife is rich. Aquatic and waterside plants grow in great profusion together with a great range of butterflies, dragonflies and other wetland invertebrates. Birdlife, too, is prolific, including unusual species with strongholds in the region and vast numbers of migrant and wintering birds. Among this wealth of wildlife are species common in other parts of Britain. There are, however, representatives from almost all major plant and animal groups that are unique, or nearly so, to the Norfolk Broads.

Man has always had a profound influence on the landscape and ecology of the Norfolk Broads and, indeed, many aspects of the Broads are entirely man-made. Their origins probably date back to medieval times when turf cutters unintentionally carved out the depressions we now see as flooded Broads. Drainage channels, the maintenance of fen and marsh vegetation through cutting and grazing, and reed cutting, add to the mosaic of wetland habitats and ensure that man's influence continues to be felt to this day.

Indeed, wetland habitats, the Norfolk Broads included, are not static environments but are constantly changing. Without some degree of activity, the Broads would become clogged with vegetation, forming fenland and eventually woodland; the rich mosaic of habitats would then be lost.

Given man's long association with the region, it should not cause surprise, perhaps, that he still holds the key to the survival of the Norfolk Broads as a viable ecosystem and continuing haven for wildlife and visitors. The last couple of decades have seen a dramatic decline in the richness and variety of the region's wildlife. Armed with the knowledge of the effects that pollution and disturbance can have, let us hope that the next 20 years may see the Broads restored to their former glory by positive conservation measures.

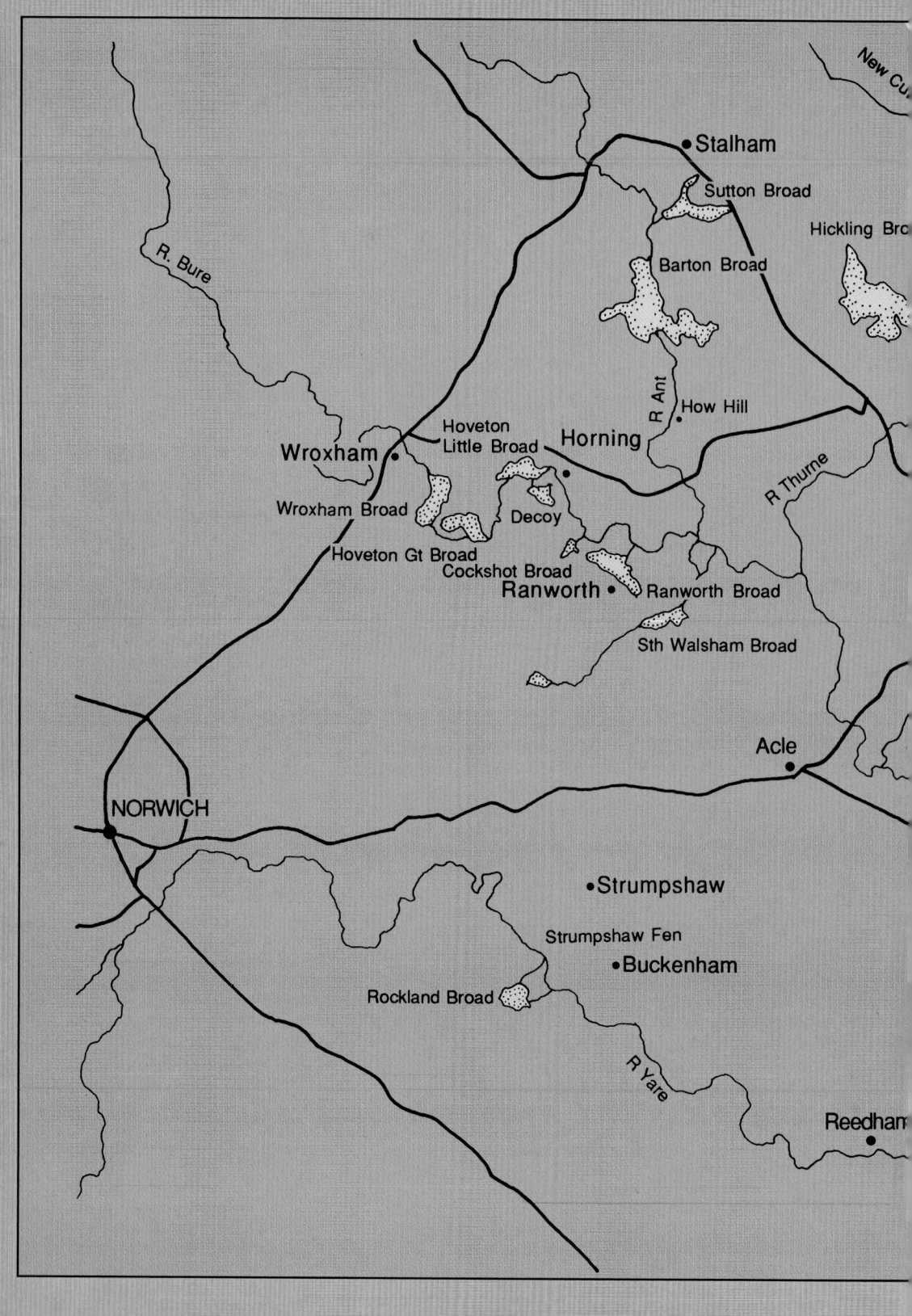

MAP OF THE
NORFOLK BROADS

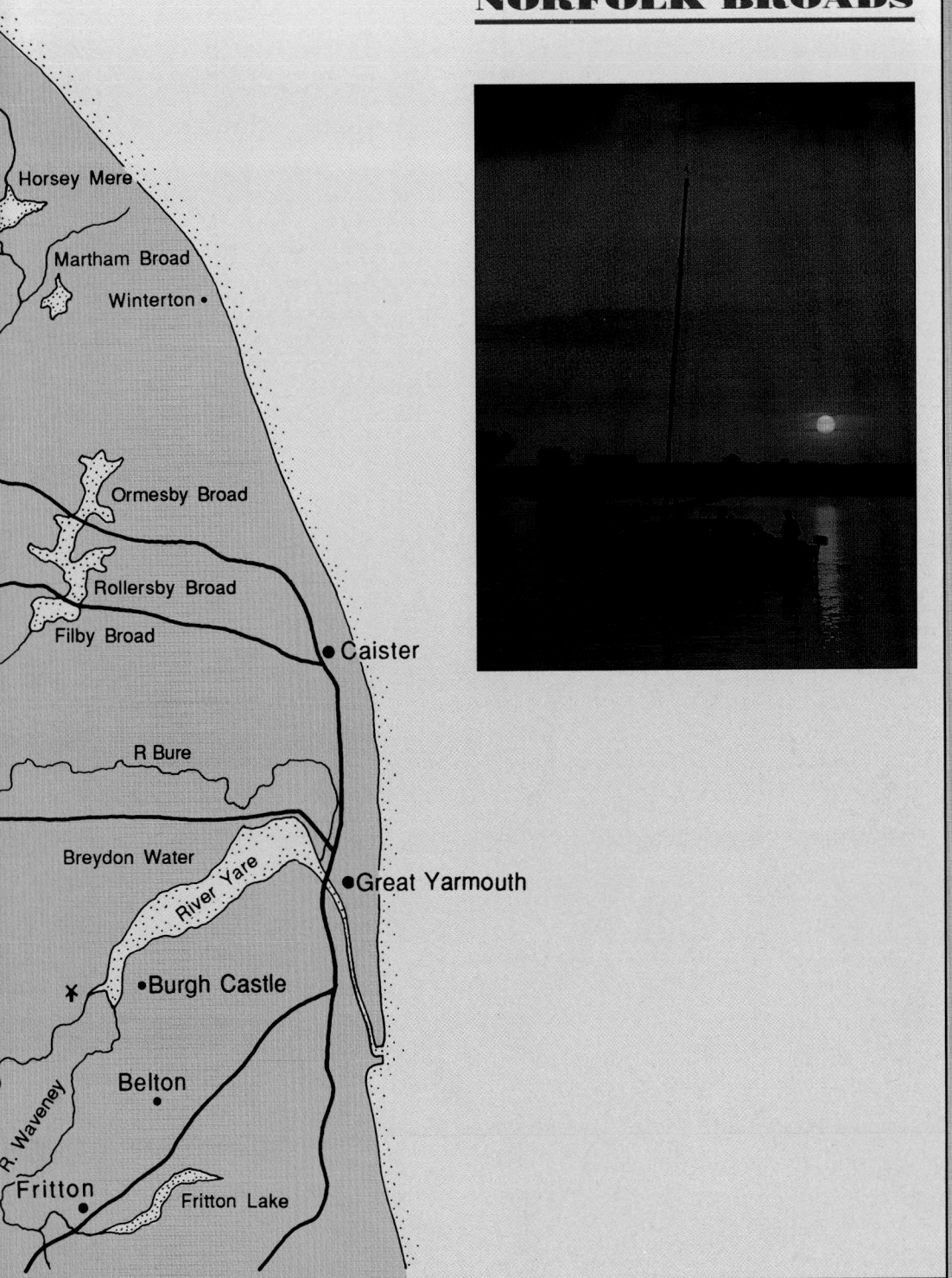

Horsey Mere

Martham Broad

Winterton •

Ormesby Broad

Rollersby Broad

Filby Broad

● Caister

R Bure

Breydon Water

River Yare

●Great Yarmouth

●Burgh Castle

R. Waveney

Belton

Fritton

Fritton Lake

*Read any book about the wildlife
of the Norfolk Broads and you will come
across a range of different habitats
described in passing in the text.
You will soon discover that, from
a wildlife point of view, a wetland is
not simply a uniform environment but
comprises a range of differing habitats.*

At first, the distinctions may seem rather
arbitrary and unimportant.
However, numerous species of plants and
animals have rigid requirements that restrict
them to one particular habitat.
A knowledge of the habitat distinctions
is of interest in its own right but can also help
the visitor in search of a particular species.

Left to their own devices, wetland habitats do not stay the same for ever. Rather, a progression can be observed from open water through colonisation by aquatic plants to the habitat becoming swamp or fenland, the final stage being carr woodland. The beauty of the Norfolk Broads is that all these habitats can be seen with ease and often side by side. The juxtaposition of habitats and the resultant mosaic is due, in no small way, to the actions of man. Curiously, while waterway clearance, land drainage, flooding, grazing and vegetation cutting all adversely affect some aspects of the environment, they also have

positive roles to play in the preservation of the Broads and the conservation of its wildlife.

The starting point for a discussion of broadland habitats begins with the open water. Even this habitat, however, needs further elaboration. Some plants and animals live at the surface while others, including many of the fish species, inhabit the water column. An additional refuge is provided by the sediment at the bottom of the water which harbours vast numbers of aquatic invertebrates, a food chain within itself, but also a resource exploited by fish from the water column above.

From the average naturalist's point of view, it is the water margins that offer most opportunities for observation. It is here that emergent vegetation proliferates, aquatic insects emerge to an adult life, and where terrestrial creatures interact with the water: birds come to feed and drink at the water's edge and many find the comparative safety of waterside vegetation ideal for nesting.

The inevitable consequence of uncontrolled growth by aquatic plants is the laying down of silt and the creation of marshes and swamps. Common reeds, such a feature of the region, form large stands of vast reedbeds and indeed the plant is often encouraged to spread by man. So important is this habitat that it is worthy of a mention of its own: birds such as bitterns and bearded tits are effectively confined to large reedbeds and this habitat even harbours rare species of moths.

Areas of wetland growing on soils which are permanently waterlogged and occasionally inundated, give rise to fens and marshes where water-loving plants thrive. Grazing and cutting obviously disadvantages more vigorous species while favouring plants such as orchids that cannot tolerate excessive competition. The pattern of land use and management greatly influences the species structure of the fenland in question.

The final progressive stage of colonisation of water by vegetation is woodland. In wetland areas, such as the Norfolk Broads, this is often referred to as carr woodland with one species in particular — alder — often dominating. Able to tolerate waterlogged soils, this tree often grows alongside shallow water but it is only in areas where the soils have become much drier that ash and birch begin to encroach.

The species described and illustrated in this book have been arranged in an order which follows the convention of relevant field guides to the region.

The selection is a mixture of the most characteristic and conspicuous members of the community together with specialities of the region. Species that are likely to arouse the curiosity of the visitor have also been included.

Where appropriate, the species average length (L.) or height (H.) is given after the Latin name. Other measurements which may help identification are incorporated into the text.

BIRDS

1 **Great Crested Grebe** *Podiceps cristatus* (L. 50cm)
This elegant waterbird is a fairly common sight as it cruises in a stately manner along the larger waterbodies of the Norfolk Broads. The great crested grebe is superbly adapted to water and seldom ventures on land where it would be vulnerable. It dives well and has a diet consisting largely of fish. In the spring, the birds develop black-and-chestnut tufts and crests on their heads, which are used in display. These are seen to best effect when pairs display to one another, sometimes standing almost upright in the water and holding water weeds in their bills.

2 **Little Grebe** *Tachybaptus ruficollis* (L. 25cm)
The dumpy little grebe is usually more common as a winter visitor to the Norfolk Broads than in summer; its trilling call is a characteristic sound in many parts of the region. During the summer months, the little grebe has chestnut on the cheeks and neck, and a lime-green patch at the base of the bill. By contrast, in winter its appearance is rather drab with grey-brown upperparts and pale underparts. Little grebes spend their entire lives associated with water. They even build floating nests of water weed which they anchor away from land and hence out of reach of many predators.

3 **Bittern** *Botaurus stellaris* (L. 75cm)
Once a common sound among larger reedbeds in the Norfolk Broads, the booming call of the bittern is now comparatively rare. Visit somewhere like Hickling Broad at dawn or dusk in the spring, however, and you still stand a chance of hearing this extraordinary sound; East Anglia is this species' last remaining stronghold in Britain. Bitterns are heron-like birds whose mottled brown plumage and upright stance affords them superb camouflage in their reedbed habitat. They stalk among the vegetation in search of prey such as eels and frogs, and are not averse to taking small mammals if the opportunity arises.

4 **Grey Heron** *Ardea cinerea* (L. 95cm)
Grey herons are past masters in the art of patient fishing. They sometimes stand completely motionless for minutes on end, waiting for a fish to swim to within striking range of their powerful, dagger-like bill. As the name suggests, the bird has largely grey plumage with a whitish neck and black cap. Long plumage on the neck and crown are particularly noticeable during the breeding season which can start as early as March. Grey herons usually nest in loose colonies, building large constructions of twigs and sticks among the branches.

5 **Spoonbill** *Platalea leucorodia* (L. 88cm)
With its huge bill shaped like a flattened spoon, and its all-white plumage, the spoonbill is an unmistakable bird when seen at close range. Although it does not breed in Britain, visiting birds from mainland Europe are sufficiently regular and usually long-staying visitors to East Anglia for many birdwatchers to be able to see them. Spoonbills feed by wading in shallow water and sweeping the bill from side to side to filter out tiny food particles from the water. In flight, the birds are also distinctive, holding both the legs and neck outstretched.

6 **Mute Swan** *Cygnus olor* (L. 150cm)
The mute swan is by far the commonest of the three species
of swan that can be seen on the Norfolk Broads and the only
one which is a year-round resident. It is an unmistakable bird
on account of its large size, orange-and-black bill and all-white
adult plumage. Immature birds are buffish in colour but
invariably associate with adult swans and share the same
characteristic S-shaped neck when swimming. As their name
suggests, mute swans are comparatively silent but nesting
birds will hiss loudly at intruders into their territory and the
wings produce a deep humming sound in flight.

9 Canada Goose *Branta canadensis* (L. 95cm)
Although introduced to this country from North America, the Canada goose is now firmly established as a breeding species. Small to medium-sized flocks are not an uncommon sight in the Broads, both on the water and feeding on adjacent farmland. The Canada goose has grey-brown plumage with a black neck and a conspicuous white cheek. In flight, which is often in a loose V formation, they make a loud honking call. In the spring, pairs nest beside large waterbodies and vigorously defend their eggs and offspring against potential predators — including man.

7 Bewick's Swan *Cygnus columbianus* (L. 122cm)
Compared to the mute swan, Bewick's swan is a much smaller bird with a proportionately shorter neck. The bill is mostly black with a relatively small but conspicuous yellow patch at the base; unlike the mute swan's bill, that of the Bewick's swan lacks the dark knob on the upper surface. This species is an autumn and winter visitor to the Norfolk Broads in small numbers. It breeds in the high Arctic and seldom arrives in Britain before October. Some of the birds seen in the Broads in autumn remain for the winter, but most pause for just a few days before continuing their journey south and west.

8 Whooper Swan *Cygnus cygnus* (L. 155cm)
Although superficially similar to Bewick's swan, a whooper is a much larger bird with a proportionately longer neck. The bill is also relatively larger and triangular in outline. It is black with yellow at the base, but in this species the yellow extends as a wedge beyond the nostrils. Whooper swans are winter visitors to Britain and are seen in the Broads from October to March; Horsey Mere and Hickling Broad are likely places to look for this species. The birds often migrate and spend the winter in family groups, the two white adult birds being accompanied by two or three buffish immature birds.

10

11

Areas of grazing marsh can be found between Ipswich and Great Yarmouth at Buckenham.

Among the birds that visit this area in the winter months are a small flock of bean geese, the only ones which regularly occur in this country. Bean geese are superficially similar to other closely related grey geese found in the region — greylag and pink-footed geese. However, when seen well, the orange feet and orange patch on the bill are diagnostic. There is a hide for viewing them, owned by the RSPB, grid reference TG 342067.

Top: Pink-footed Goose Anser brachyrhynchus
Bottom: Bean Goose Anser fabilis

10 **Greylag Goose** *Anser anser* (L. 85cm)
As a truly wild bird, the greylag goose is a rather rare visitor to the Norfolk Broads. However, a sizeable feral population exists in East Anglia and birds of domestic ancestry are not an uncommon sight. The greylag is a large and stoutly built goose with mainly grey plumage; there are darker streaks on the neck and barring on the flanks and back. The legs are pink and the bill is a uniform orange-pink. The greylag is a fairly noisy bird. It utters a range of honks and nasal barks recalling sounds made by domestic geese, which are descendants of the greylag.

11 **White-fronted Goose** *Anser albifrons* (L. 70cm)
The white-fronted goose is a winter visitor to the Norfolk Broads from its Arctic breeding ground. Small numbers arrive in October or November and stay until March; larger numbers occasionally appear if harsh winter weather forces flocks to leave the feeding grounds on mainland Europe. White-fronted geese have mainly grey-brown plumage with dark barring on the belly, and orange legs. The race that visits East Anglia has a pinkish bill and adults have a conspicuous white patch on the forehead from which their name derives. Flocks are usually seen feeding on arable land.

12 Mallard *Anas platyrhynchos* (L. 60cm)
The commonest duck in the Norfolk Broads. It is present throughout the year, although numbers build up in the autumn, boosted by migrants from the continent. The male's green-glossed head, chestnut breast and grey-brown plumage make him distinctive, while the female is a more uniform mottled brown in colour. In flight, both sexes show a broad, blue band — called a speculum — on the trailing edge of the wing. Mallards are dabbling ducks and feed by up-ending in shallow water to feed on seeds and other organic matter in the mud. The female makes a loud quacking call.

13 Gadwall *Anas strepera* (L. 50cm)
Seen at close range, the male gadwall is a most attractive bird — despite its largely grey-brown plumage. It has incredibly fine and intricate vermiculations on the feathering of its breast and flanks in particular. The undertail feathers are black and often show up very well through binoculars; in flight, both sexes show deep-red wing panels and a white speculum making them easy to identify. The female is rather similar to a female mallard and is best told by her association with the male. Gadwalls are mainly winter visitors to the Broads.

14 Pintail *Anas acuta* (L. 60cm)
The most distinctive features of the pintail are the elongated central tail feathers of the male which give this species its name. The drake is a striking-looking bird with a rich brown head and white neck. When seen swimming, the soft grey markings on the flanks are separated from the black undertail by a white band. The female is mottled brown but shares the male's same accentuated tail-end, although the tail feathers are not nearly so elongated. Pintails are usually seen in pairs and are rather scarce winter visitors to the region, both to the Broads and to neighbouring coasts.

15 Wigeon *Anas penelope* (L. 45cm)
At a distance, a flock of wigeon can be easily identified by their distinctive whistling 'wheeeooo' calls. This duck is a winter visitor to the Norfolk Broads region. Although it is seen on the Broads themselves, it usually prefers more saline conditions as are found at Breydon Water and on the coast itself. The male has an orange head with a yellow crown; the breast is pinkish, the flanks and back are grey and the undertail shows black bordered with white. The female is reddish brown and is best told by shape and association with the male. In flight, both sexes show a lot of white on the forewing.

16 Teal *Anas crecca* (L. 35cm)
The teal is the smallest species of duck found in Britain and is common in the Norfolk Broads on autumn migration and as a winter visitor. The male has finely marked grey-brown plumage with an orange head and green through the eye. Under certain circumstances, the buffish-yellow undertail and white flank stripe are conspicuous. The female is mottled brown and is best told by her small size and association with the male. Teal sometimes feed by up-ending in shallow water, but also graze on grassland, sometimes mixing with other ducks and waders.

17 Garganey *Anan querquedula* (L. 38cm)
Very small numbers of garganey breed in the Norfolk Broads but this species is mainly seen on migration, and then mostly in the spring. The presence of the male is often first detected by its peculiar, rattling call. A good view reveals a brown head with a distinctive white stripe over the eye; the rest of the plumage is a mixture of brown, grey-brown and white and, in flight, the forewings are pale blue. The female is mottled brown but shows the same wing pattern as the male in flight. Were it not for these markings, she could be confused with a female teal.

18 **Shoveler** *Anas clypeata* (L. 50cm)
Aptly named for its long, spoon-shaped bill, the shoveler is one of the most distinctive species of ducks. The male has a shiny green head and reddish-chestnut belly and flanks, bordered on the breast and undertail by white. The back is brownish and, in flight, the forewings are pale blue. The female is mottled brown but can usually be told by the shape of the bill alone. Shovelers feed in shallow water using their strange bills to filter out small organic particles from the mud. They are resident in the Norfolk Broads with numbers being swollen in autumn and winter by continental visitors.

19 **Shelduck** *Tadorna tadorna* (L 60cm)
The shelduck mostly favours coastal habitats and tidal reaches such as Breydon Water, rather than the freshwater Broads themselves. It is a large and distinctive duck, the sexes of which are very similar. At a distance it looks mainly black and white but a closer view reveals a glossy black head, chestnut breast band and black flight feathers and scapulars on otherwise white plumage. The bill is red and the legs pinkish. Shelducks are burrow-nesters in sand dunes around the coast. In the winter, they are usually seen in small flocks.

20 **Scaup** *Aythya marila* (L. 45cm)
If the winter weather turns particularly severe then small flocks of scaup occasionally appear on ice-free waters in the Norfolk Broads. Otherwise, small flocks are usually found on coastal waters in the region. Scaup are most easily confused with tufted ducks, to which they are closely related. The male has a glossy-black head, neck and breast, white underparts and a soft-grey back, the latter feature the best for separation from the male tufted duck. Female scaups are brown, their best identification feature being the large white patch at the base of the bill. Scaup are diving ducks, spending long periods submerged.

21 Tufted Duck *Aythya fuligula* (L. 43cm)

Tufted ducks are regular and fairly common winter visitors to the Norfolk Broads, preferring larger areas of open water and sometimes rivers. The male appears mostly black and white at a distance. The head has a tufted outline and, at close range, a purplish gloss can be seen. The female is mostly brown but shows the suggestion of a tuft and a small white patch at the base of the bill. Tufted ducks feed on aquatic invertebrates which are caught by diving. This species is usually seen in flocks, sometimes in the company of pochards and other ducks.

22 Pochard *Aythya ferina* (L. 45cm)

A few pairs of pochards breed in the region but the species is much more common and widespread in the winter, large areas of open water such as Hickling Broad and Horsey Mere often being particularly favoured. The male has attractive plumage with an orange-red head, black breast and vent, white underparts and soft grey back. The female has grey-brown plumage but often shows a rather conspicuous pale spectacle marking around the eye. Pochards are diving ducks and are usually seen in small flocks. In flight the wings look pale grey-brown above and whitish below.

23 Goldeneye *Bucephala clangula* (L. 48cm)

Although a few goldeneye breed in Scotland, most nest in northern Europe and visit Britain as winter visitors. The species is fairly common around the coast of East Anglia and, in harsh winter weather in particular, occurs on waterways and lakes in the Norfolk Broads. The male is distinctive with a large, rounded dark head bearing a conspicuous white patch near the base of the bill; the back is dark and the underparts white. Female goldeneyes have an orange-red head and otherwise grey-brown plumage. Both sexes have yellow eyes and large white patches on the wings.

24 Smew *Mergus albellus* (L. 40cm)

A male smew is one of the most attractive and distinctive of all ducks. The plumage is essentially white, and bold black lines and a dark smudge through the eye add to the striking appearance. By comparison, the female is rather drab, having grey-brown plumage with white cheeks and a reddish cap on the head. Smew are diving ducks which feed on fish. They are winter visitors to Britain and usually turn up in the Norfolk Broads during spells of particularly harsh weather, fairly late in the winter. Juveniles, which resemble females, often predominate among the sightings.

25 **Goosander** *Mergus merganser*
(L. 65cm)
Winter is the time of year to look for
goosanders in the Norfolk Broads.
These streamlined, fish-eating ducks
occur in small numbers between October
and March, and prefer larger areas of
open water. Males are distinctive birds.
The head is dark, but appears glossy-
green in good light while the rest of the
body is mostly white tinged with pink,
except for the dark back. The female has
grey-brown plumage and an orange-brown
head. Both sexes have relatively thin,
reddish bills, the margins of which are
serrated. In flight, males in particular
show a considerable amount of white on
the inner wings.

26 **Kestrel** *Falco tinnunculus* (L. 34cm)
The kestrel is the commonest and most
widespread bird of prey in the Norfolk
Broads region, and indeed in Britain as a
whole. It characteristically and frequently
hovers, scanning the ground below for
prey such as small mammals. This feat is
often performed over roadside verges,
but in the Norfolk Broads reedbeds also
offer good hunting grounds. The sexes
have different plumages. In the male the
head and tail are greyish, the latter with a
dark terminal band, while the back and
inner wings are chestnut and the wing
tips black. Females are a more uniform
brown, darker above than below.

27 **Marsh Harrier** *Circus aeruginosus* (L. 50cm)
Few birds of prey are more habitat specific than the marsh harrier, which feeds and nests almost exclusively in the extensive reedbeds that fringe many of the Broads. Their flight pattern is very distinctive: broad wings and a long tail enable them to fly slowly, a few feet above the reeds, dropping down if they locate prey. Females are larger than males and have mostly dark brown plumage but with pale brown on the crown, throat and forewing. Males are reddish-brown with greyish wings and tail and black wingtips. Marsh harriers are mostly summer visitors to the Norfolk Broads.

28 **Pheasant** *Phasianus colchicus* (L. 80cm)
Although introduced to this country from Asia for hunting, pheasants are now well established throughout Britain and a colourful addition to the birdlife of the Norfolk Broads region. The male has shiny orange-brown plumage with an iridescent blue-green head and a red wattle. Females are sandy brown and mottled and both sexes have long, barred tails. Pheasants are often seen feeding in arable fields during the winter months, roosting in hedgerow trees and woods at night. The loud, explosive call of the male is a familiar sound.

29 **Water Rail** *Rallus aquaticus* (L. 28cm)
Sounding more like a squealing pig than a bird, the far-carrying call of the water rail is a familiar sound in the Norfolk Broads. These brown-and-grey water birds have long, red bills and long legs and toes, the latter features ideally suiting them to a life in marshy environments. Reedbeds and damp woodlands are typical water rail habitats, the birds being generally more widespread and common in the winter than in the summer. They are usually more often heard than seen, being rather shy, but harsh winter weather sometimes forces them to feed in the open.

26

POLLUTION

Over the last few decades, the Norfolk Broads have been discovered as an accessible playground for British holidaymakers.

People are drawn to the area who enjoy boating, fishing, birdwatching and just plain relaxation. It is one of the great ironies of tourism that increased numbers of visitors to an area invariably leads to a deterioration in the very qualities that made it attractive in the first place.
This holds true in the Norfolk Broads. Powered boats inevitably have minor fuel spills from time to time and boats of all kinds can cause physical damage to fragile marginal habitats. Lead fishing weights have caused heavy metal poisoning in wildfowl, and tourists of all denominations leave litter. Thankfully, it is now recognised that a dilemma exists and steps are being taken to address the problem.

30 Coot *Fulica atra* (L. 38cm)

Coots are common and widespread throughout the waterways of the Norfolk Broads all year round. In the winter months, their numbers are boosted by influxes of continental birds arriving here to escape the harsh winters. Coots are distinctive, all-black birds with prominent white bills which extend up the forecrown as a white plate. Their long, lobed toes are ideal both for swimming and for walking on floating vegetation. Young coots have spiky feathers and almost bald, red-and-yellow heads.

31 Moorhen *Gallinula chloropus* (L. 33cm)

Swimming with jerky movements and a flicking tail, the moorhen is an extremely common resident of watery habitats in the Norfolk Broads. Adult birds have rich-brown upperparts and dark-grey underparts. The yellow-tipped red bill and frontal shield are characteristic, as are the yellow-green legs with long toes. When swimming, moorhens show a white stripe along the flanks and white on the undertail. In flight, the wings look broad and the legs and feet are dangling. At the start of the breeding season, male moorhens behave aggressively and do battle with one another.

32 Lapwing *Vanellus vanellus* (L. 30cm)

Grasslands, arable fields and marshes offer nesting sites to that elegant wader, the lapwing. In spring, their loud 'pee-wit' calls can be heard as the birds fly overhead on rounded, black-and-white wings, mobbing intruders into their territories. When seen in good light, the lapwing has a greenish sheen to the feathers of its back, and a long, thin crest that often catches in the wind. Three or four well-camouflaged eggs are laid in a simple scrape in the ground. Outside the breeding season, lapwings are often seen in flocks which sometimes number 100 birds or more.

33 Oystercatcher *Haematopus ostralegus* (L. 43cm)

In East Anglia, the oystercatcher is mainly a bird of the coast although a few birds occasionally visit the marshes to feed and bathe. It is a particularly striking bird with mainly black upperparts, white underparts and a prominent white wingbar seen in flight. Equally noticeable are the long, bright red bill and the pink legs. Oystercatchers nest on shingle and sandy beaches, laying their eggs in a simple scrape in the ground. Not surprisingly, human disturbance excludes them from many areas of coastline. They feed by probing for invertebrates but also use their bill to chisel molluscs off rocks.

34 Ringed Plover *Charadrius hiaticula* (L. 18cm)

The ringed plover is present throughout the year in the Norfolk Broads region. Although it is seen mostly around the coast or along tidal stretches such as Breydon Water, it is not unusual to see the occasional bird beside freshwater inland from the coast. Ringed plovers are small, dumpy waders with short necks, rounded heads and relatively short bills. The upperparts are sandy brown, the underparts white and head and throat have bold black markings. Ringed plovers feed in a characteristic manner by running along the ground, pausing and then bending down to pick up an item of food. They make a soft 'tu-eep' call.

35 Turnstone *Arenaria interpres* (L. 23cm)

Mottled plumage affords the turnstone excellent camouflage as its feeds unobtrusively along the shoreline, or occasionally at watery margins on Hickling Broad or Breydon Water. It is a rather dumpy wader with a short, triangular bill, used like a chisel to turn stones and weed in search of invertebrates such as sandhoppers. Turnstones nest in the Arctic and visit Britain as non-breeding visitors from October to March. They are usually seen in small groups which, when disturbed, fly off revealing white on the wings and back, and uttering a loud 'tu-kek-kek' call.

30

31

36 Grey Plover

Pluvialis squatarola (L. 29cm)
The grey plover is almost
exclusively a bird of the coast,
favouring estuaries and mudflats
at areas like Breydon Water. It is
a winter visitor and passage
migrant to the region, mainly
from October to March. In
summer plumage, only seen
briefly in this country, the
underparts are jet black. For the
rest of the year, the bird has
spangled grey upperparts and
pale underparts. Grey plovers
have dark legs and a short, dark
bill; they feed by picking small
animals from the surface of the
mud. A useful identification
feature is the black 'armpit', best
seen in flight, and the diagnostic
call which sounds like a human
wolf-whistle.

37 Golden Plover

Pluvialis apricaria (L. 27cm)
When seen in good light, the
golden plover is a most
attractive bird. During the winter
months, when it occurs most
regularly in the Norfolk Broads,
it has golden spangled
upperparts and pale buff
underparts. Golden plovers are
invariably seen in flocks, usually
feeding on ploughed fields and
grassland. They are relatively
nervous birds and often take to
the wing, revealing their white
underwings. Flocks often feed
alongside, and mix with, flocks
of lapwings. Golden plovers
breed in upland Britain and visit
the Norfolk Broads between late
September and April.

38 Dunlin *Calidris alpina* (L. 18cm)

The dunlin is seen in the Norfolk Broads region as a passage migrant in spring and autumn and as a winter visitor. It is a sociable bird and invariably seen in flocks feeding on mudflats and estuaries in the area. It does, however, sometimes occur in small numbers on marshes and wetlands in the Norfolk Broads as well. The dunlin is the most numerous small wader in Europe and also one of the most variable in appearance. Bill length varies tremendously from individual to individual and plumage ranges from largely grey and white in the winter to chestnut upperparts, pale, streaked underparts and a black belly in summer.

39 Knot *Calidris canutus* (L. 25cm)

Because in its non-breeding season the knot lacks any striking or diagnostic markings, it can be a difficult bird to identify at first glance. Adults in winter have rather greyish plumage with paler underparts; the legs are yellowish and the bill is dark, straight and relatively short. Juvenile birds, seen in the autumn, are similar but have a warm, buffish wash to the plumage. Knots are birds of the coast, preferring the mudflats of Breydon Water to neighbouring freshwater areas. In suitable locations, they are seen in flocks which fly and roost in tight-packed formation.

40 Snipe *Gallinago gallinago* (L. 25cm)

Few birds can be so easily identified from silhouette alone as the snipe: the immensely long, straight bill, dumpy body and relatively short legs are quite characteristic. Seen in good light, the snipe has beautiful feathering, the upperparts being a mixture of chestnut, black and white and the underparts having strong barring. The head has bold, black stripes and the eye is large and curiously positioned. Snipe are year-round residents in the Norfolk Broads, preferring marshy wetlands and shallow freshwater for feeding. Their numbers increase in winter, however, due to immigrants from northern Europe.

HICKLING BROAD

A permit is needed to visit this nature reserve run by the Norfolk Naturalists' Trust; this can be obtained from the warden's office in Hickling.

It is well worth the effort of obtaining one, and the site has something to offer all year round. All the classic broadland reedbed birds are here, including bearded tits, bitterns and marsh harriers. Wildfowl and waders are numerous in appropriate seasons and the wetland plantlife is superb. There is even a good colony of swallowtail butterflies.

Cowbane Cicuta virosa

41 **Green Sandpiper** *Tringa ochropus* (L. 23cm)
If you disturb a small wader from a marsh or wet ditch in winter and it flies off revealing a white rump, then it is almost certain to be a green sandpiper. Winter visitors to Britain, these attractive little waders have rather dark upperparts and contrasting white underparts. When feeding in shallow water, they characteristically bob up and down and when alarmed utter a loud 'tluee-tluee-tluee' call. Green sandpipers are rather solitary in their habits but a few may be seen together in suitable broadland habitats. They are present from October to March in most years.

42 **Greenshank** *Tringa nebularia* (L. 31cm)
Spring and autumn are the seasons to look for greenshank in the Norfolk Broads region. These elegant waders breed in northern Europe, including Scotland, but winter mostly in Africa; the marshlands of East Anglia make an ideal stopping-off point for feeding and resting. Greenshank have rather grey-brown upperparts and paler underparts; at a distance they can look very pale indeed. The bill is long and slightly upturned and the legs are long and yellowish-green. They are rather nervous birds and take to the wing with a loud 'teu-teu-teu' call.

43 **Redshank** *Tringa totanus* (L. 27cm)
A shrill alarm call, uttered at intruders, has earned the redshank the nickname 'watchdog of the marshes'. It is a common bird in the Norfolk Broads region throughout the

year, breeding on the marshes and feeding in shallow pools and estuaries. An influx of migrants boosts winter numbers making this bird easy to see. As their name implies, redshank have striking red legs and a long, straight bill which is red at the base. The plumage is brown with darker markings during the breeding season, but becoming a more uniform grey-brown in the winter.

44 **Ruff** *Philomachus pugnax* (L. 30cm)
Once common as a breeding species, the ruff is now seen mainly during spring and autumn migration at marshy wetlands such as Hickling Broad. In the spring, male ruffs acquire showy ruffs and ear tufts that can be white, black or orange-brown, or indeed any shade in between. The feathering is used in ritualised displays which can sometimes be seen in the region. Females — called reeves — are considerably smaller than males and lack the showy feathering on the head; their plumage is largely grey-brown with irregularly placed dark feathers on the back.

45 **Avocet** *Recurvirostra avosetta* (L. 43cm)
Few birds can be more distinctive and readily identified than the avocet. With its black and white plumage, long bluish legs, and long, upturned bill, it is unlikely to be confused with any other bird in the region. Once extinct in this country as a breeding bird, efforts by the RSPB and other conservation organisations have resulted in their being a common sight at coastal reserves in north Norfolk and Suffolk.

As a consequence, it is not at all unusual to see avocets in the Norfolk Broads region, in areas where shallow, coastal pools provide ideal conditions for feeding.

46 **Black-headed Gull** *Larus ridibundus* (L. 36cm)
The black-headed gull is by far the most common gull species to be seen in the region. Small colonies breed within the Norfolk Broads and much larger colonies can be found along the north Norfolk coast. During the summer months, adults have a dark, chocolate-brown hood which is lost during the winter. At all times of the year the upperparts are pale grey and the underparts are white. In flight, this species shows a diagnostic white leading edge to the wings. Black-headed gulls are very adaptable and soon learn to take food from man at car parks and coastal resorts.

47 **Herring Gull** *Larus argentatus* (L. 56cm)
Seen side by side, the herring gull is noticeably larger than the black-headed gull. It has grey upperparts, white underparts and black wingtips, most noticeable in flight. At close range, the pink legs can be seen, as can the stout yellow bill with an orange spot near the tip. Herring gulls are more numerous in the region during the winter months. They often visit the Broads to bathe and preen, having spent the day feeding on ploughed fields nearby. Herring gulls are also fairly common along the coast, especially near resorts where they can scavenge for scraps of food.

48 **Common Tern** *Sterna hirundo* (L. 35cm)
The common tern is a summer visitor to the Norfolk Broads region, arriving in May and leaving again in September. Of the several tern species to be encountered here, this is by far the commonest. It can be recognised by its graceful flight and pale plumage, slightly greyer above than below. At close range, the dagger-like bill, which is bright red with a black tip, can be seen, along with the short red legs. Large colonies of common terns can be found along the north Norfolk coast and the species occasionally nests here in small numbers. Most, however, are seen around the coast or over open water, feeding by plunge-diving after small fish.

49 **Woodpigeon** *Columba palumbus* (L. 40cm)
Seen throughout the year, the woodpigeon is an extremely common resident of the Norfolk Broads region. Although not typically associated with the Broads themselves, they are most abundant in the surrounding farmland, woodland and hedgerows. Woodpigeons are usually seen in flocks which, during the winter months, can be quite sizeable. They have mostly grey-brown plumage with a reddish breast. There are patches of white and shiny green feathering on the sides of the neck and, in flight, prominent transverse white wing bars can be clearly seen.

50 **Cuckoo** *Cuculus canorus* (L. 33cm)
Heralding the arrival of spring, the cuckoo's song can be heard as early as the third week in April. In flight, the cuckoo is superficially similar to a sparrowhawk, a fact that incites small songbirds to mob it. Another reason for this antipathy may be the cuckoo's parasitic egg-laying habits — it lays its own in that of dunnocks, reed warblers and other small birds, leaving them to rear the young. Seen well, cuckoos have mostly grey plumage but with pale, barred underparts. Immature birds and a small proportion of females are reddish brown.

51 **Short-eared Owl** *Asio flammeus* (L. 38cm)
Being largely diurnal in its habits, the short-eared owl is regularly encountered by birdwatchers. This species hunts for small mammals such as voles and small birds, and can be seen quartering fields and marshes in search of prey. Short-eared owls are seen as passage migrants through the region, as well as winter visitors and occasional summer residents. At close range, the staring yellow eyes are noticeable. They are seen mostly, however, at a distance in flight when the long, rounded wings and buoyant flight are seen to good effect. Short-eared owls also occasionally perch on prominent fence posts.

52 **Swift** *Apus apus* (L. 17cm)
Late May and early June sees the arrival of swifts to Britain from their wintering grounds in Africa. These fast-flying aerial masters are insect-feeders, catching their food on the wing. In the Norfolk Broads region they are a common sight, often in considerable numbers, over areas of open water and marsh; their numbers tend to build up towards the end of the day as aquatic insects take to the wing. Swifts nest in the roofs of houses. This is the only time in their lives not spent on the wing. Although their swept-back, sickle-shaped wings may suit them to a life in flight, they are ill-adapted to walking and can barely shuffle along.

53 **Kingfisher** *Alcedo atthis* (L. 18cm)
The kingfisher surely ranks as Britain's most colourful bird: with its orange-red breast and blue and green, iridescent upperparts, it has a most striking appearance. Kingfishers are fairly common in the Norfolk Broads region, nesting in burrows excavated in banks beside water. Vigilant observers may be lucky enough to see one perched on an overhanging branch or reed stem. Most people, however, simply see a flash of electric blue as a kingfisher flies low over the water uttering its sharp call. Kingfishers feed by plunge-diving for small fish such as minnows.

54 Great Spotted Woodpecker *Dendrocopus major* (L. 23cm)

Areas of woodland, including relatively small patches of damp alder carr, are home to the great spotted woodpecker. This is the most common of the three British species of woodpecker and the one most likely to be encountered in the Norfolk Broads region. Birdwatchers are often first alerted to its presence by the loud 'kik' call uttered in alarm. A close view reveals largely black-and-white plumage, with prominent white patches and barring on the wings. Males have red on the nape, a feature which is lacking in females; immature birds have a reddish crown.

55 Swallow *Hirundo rustica* (L. 19cm)

Swallows are insect-eating birds that feed on the wing. It is not surprising, therefore, that they are extremely common almost everywhere in the Norfolk Broads, given the abundance of insect life to be found there. The first swallows may arrive in late March but most arrive a month or so later. They nest in outbuildings throughout the region and feed over open water and marshes. They share the air over the Broads with other similar birds; swallows can, however, always be recognised by their deeply forked tails. Just prior to migration in September, huge numbers of swallows gather in the region, roosting at night in the reedbeds.

56 House Martin *Delichon urbica* (L. 14cm)
It is not uncommon to see rows of the cup-shaped mud nests of house martins adorning the eaves of houses and cottages in the Norfolk Broads region. These endearing summer visitors arrive in April and can be seen gathering mud from puddles and hawking for insects over the open Broads and associated reedbeds. House martins have largely blue-black upperparts and white underparts; their most distinctive feature, however, is the white rump, best seen in flight. In the autumn, house martins occasionally gather with swallows and sand martins, hundreds sometimes perched together on overhead wires.

57 Sand Martin *Riparia riparia* (L. 13cm)
Sandy cliffs around the Norfolk coast and vertical cliffs in sandpits provide ideal nesting sites for the sand martin. These summer visitors to the region breed colonially, excavating nest burrows in the loose substrate. Sand martins can be recognised by their sandy-brown upperparts and pale underparts. A good view of one in flight will reveal the diagnostic band across the throat and upper breast. They feed on insects which are caught on the wing in the manner of swallows and house martins. In the autumn, all three species often gather together in loose, mixed flocks prior to migration.

58 Yellow Wagtail *Motacilla flava* (L. 16.5cm)
The yellow wagtail is a fairly common summer visitor to the Norfolk Broads and its characteristic 'tsreet' call is a familiar sound between April and August. These delightful birds nest in grazing marshes and sometimes even arable fields; they feed on insects, sometimes following cattle through the marshes, collecting beetles and other small creatures disturbed by their progress. As their name suggests, yellow wagtails are indeed yellow and do continually pump their tail up and down. Males are more brightly coloured than females and juveniles are olive or grey-brown in colour.

BREYDON WATER

Just to the west of Great Yarmouth lies a large, inland estuary known as Breydon Water, at the mouths of the Rivers Yare and Waveney.

At low tide, the estuary empties out to reveal a vast expanse of mudflats and saltmarsh. During the winter months, there are Brent geese, shelduck, wigeon, curlew, godwits and many more species. Spring and autumn migration, from March to May and August to October respectively, is, if anything, more exciting with vast numbers of birds passing through. A network of public footpaths allows visitors to view the area.

Top: Brent Goose Branta bernicla
Bottom: Sea Milkwort Glaux maritima

59

59 Pied Wagtail *Motacilla alba yarrellii* (L. 18.5cm)
Present throughout the year in the Norfolk Broads, the pied
wagtail is a fairly common and widespread bird in the region.
Its name is extremely descriptive, for the bird is indeed pied
— black-and-white — and wags or pumps its tail. Pied
wagtails feed on insects and are often associated with
wetland areas where they feed along muddy margins. In the
winter, they can be seen roosting communally in some areas
in dense reedbeds. Pied wagtails are also birds of urban
areas and are a common sight on school playing fields or in
town parks.

60 Starling *Sturnus vulgaris* (L. 21cm)
The spectacle of thousands of starlings coming in to roost,
against a backdrop of a glowing winter sunset, is a
memorable one. Feeding in open fields and on the marshes
during the day, the birds fly to extensive reedbeds around the
Broads just as the light is fading. The starling has rather dark
plumage with an iridescent sheen and white spots in winter.
These characterful birds nest in the region in good numbers
but their population is swollen in autumn by migrants from the
continent. Starlings are also not averse to feeding on lawns or
even raiding bird tables in the winter.

61 Wren *Troglodytes troglodytes* (L. 10cm)
The wren is among the smallest birds in Britain. This
diminutive species is a common resident in the Norfolk
Broads, although the population plummets during periods of
harsh winter weather. The wren is heard more often than it is
seen. When alarmed, it makes a scolding 'tik' and it has a
rattling call. The song is very loud and musical, usually ending
in a loud trill. Wrens are insectivores, searching for insects in
the cover of hedgerows, scrub and undergrowth. With their
rich brown plumage and furtive habits, they could be mistaken
at first glance for a mouse.

62 Dunnock *Prunella modularis* (L. 15cm)
Rather retiring and skulking for most of the year, dunnocks
are most easily seen in the early spring. Males often perch
prominently and sing loudly to advertise their presence within
a territory. The song is rather musical and recalls that of a
blackcap with its rich tones and rapid warbling. The dunnock

61

is also known as the hedge sparrow, although it is unrelated
to this group of birds. It has blue-grey underparts, rich-brown
upperparts and a fine bill. One aspect of its alternative name
is apt, however: it is often found in hedgerows, but also likes
scrub and overgrown woodland.

63 Robin *Erithacus rubecula* (L. 14cm)
Few birds can be more familiar to British birdwatchers than
the robin. This engaging little bird is characterised by the
striking orange-red breast, bordered with grey, the brown
upperparts and white belly. Juveniles are typically brown with
pale teardrop spots on the upperparts. Robins are found in all
sorts of habitats in the Norfolk Broads region, but mostly in
hedgerows, gardens and woodlands. They can be heard
singing a rather plaintive song at almost any time of year,
although the nature of the tune changes with the seasons.

64 Reed Warbler *Acrocephalus scirpaceus* (L. 12.5cm)
The reed warbler is a summer visitor to Britain and is seen in
the Norfolk Broads from May to August. It is one of the most
characteristic birds of reedbeds in the region and is perhaps
better known for its song than its appearance. Often delivered
from the cover of the reeds, the song is a mixture of harsh
and tuneful phrases, each one of which is usually repeated
two or three times. Reed warblers build superbly constructed
cup-shaped nests which are attached to a few individual reed
stems and suspended out of harm's way several feet off the
ground or above the water.

60

62

63

64

65 Sedge Warbler *Acrocephalus schoenobaenus*
(L. 12.5cm)
Reed-filled ditches and overgrown marshy vegetation provide ideal habitats for the sedge warbler, a summer visitor to Britain. It is common and widespread in the Norfolk Broads between May and August and, unlike its relative the reed warbler, often sings from an elevated perch such as an isolated bush or bramble spray; occasionally, the song is delivered in flight. Sedge warblers have sandy-brown plumage, the upperparts marked with dark streaks; there is a striking, pale stripe above the eye which is easily seen on a perched bird.

66 Redwing *Turdus iliacus* (L. 20cm)
In September and October, flocks of redwings arrive on the east coast of Britain to spend the winter here. Large numbers pass through the Norfolk Broads region and many stay for the whole winter if food supplies last. Redwings are members of the thrush family. Although superficially similar to the song thrush, they have a striking white stripe above the eye and red on the flanks and underwing. They feed mainly on berries and fruit, but will also feed on the ground if food is short. They are often seen in the company of fieldfares; this is a mistle thrush-like bird with a grey head and rump, chestnut back and orange-buff breast.

67 Rook *Corvus frugilegus*
(L. 46cm)
As early as March, rooks start to congregate around their traditional, tree-top colonial rookeries in Norfolk woodlands. Twigs and branches are used to repair any damage and it is not long before the first egg is laid. Rooks have all-black plumage and are superficially similar to crows. They do, however, have long bills and bare, whitish skin at the base of the bill. Another characteristic of the rook is its tendency to be seen in flocks. During the winter months especially, they feed in ploughed fields and grassland, taking considerable numbers of insect grubs.

68 Jackdaw *Corvus monedula*
(L. 33cm)
Church towers, farm outbuildings and hollow trees provide ideal nesting sites for jackdaws. These relatively small members of the crow family are fairly common in the Norfolk Broads region although they are seldom seen over open water or reedbeds. At a distance, the plumage looks all-dark but in good light, the grey nape and pale eye can be seen. Their flight is direct and with rapid wingbeats. In some areas, jackdaws become bold and inquisitive; where they are not persecuted, they will come to car parks and villages to scavenge scraps of food.

69 Bearded Tit *Panurus biarmicus* (L. 16.5cm)
Sometimes referred to as 'pingers' on account of their thin but distinctive calls, bearded tits have one of the main British strongholds in the Norfolk Broads. They are almost exclusively confined to reedbed habitats and feed on seeds for much of the year. They can be rather difficult to see, especially if the wind is blowing the reeds. Occasionally, however, small flocks can be seen flying low over the reeds showing short, rounded wings and long tails. Seen at close range, males have a bluish head and black moustachial stripe; females are a more uniform brown.

70 Goldfinch *Carduelis carduelis* (L. 14cm)
The collective name for a flock of goldfinches is a 'charm'. This delightfully descriptive noun certainly does justice to these beautiful little birds. Their plumage is largely black, buff and white, but they have red on the face and show bright yellow on the wings in flight. To add to this appealing description, they utter tinkling calls when they take to the wing. Goldfinches are fairly common in the Norfolk Broads region. They are mostly encountered during the winter months when roaming flocks feed on riverside thistles and other seed-bearing plants.

71 Chaffinch *Fringilla coelebs* (L. 15cm)
The chaffinch is a common bird in the Norfolk Broads region
throughout the year although numbers are augmented during
the winter months by migrants from the continent. The male is
a brightly coloured bird with a pinkish breast, blue crown,
brown back and greenish rump. The female is a more uniform
buffish brown and both sexes have two striking white wing
bars. In the spring, the male sings a descending song which
ends with a final flourish. Outside the breeding season,
chaffinches are seen in flocks that feed in arable fields and
woods and roost in trees, sometimes close to water.

72 House Sparrow *Passer domesticus* (L. 14cm)
Often associated with man, the house sparrow is a common
resident in many parts of the Norfolk Broads. They often nest
in roofs and outbuildings and can be seen feeding wherever
there are good supplies of grain. Male house sparrows are
more distinctively marked than females. They have a greyish
cap, a black bib, a grey rump and brownish upperparts.
Females, on the other hand, have plainer head markings.
House sparrows are usually seen in small flocks. Keep an eye
open for the scarcer tree sparrow which has a brown cap and
white face with a distinct black patch on the ear coverts.

73 Yellowhammer *Emberiza citrinella* (L. 16.5cm)
Hedgerows and bushes on the edges of the marsh provide
ideal habitats for the yellowhammer. The male is brightly
coloured with a chestnut back and yellow head and
underparts; the female's plumage is a more washed-out
version of the male's. In the spring, male yellowhammers
perch prominently within their territory and sing their
characteristic song, often rendered 'a little bit of bread and no
cheese'. Outside the breeding season, the birds are seen in
small flocks feeding in arable fields, sometimes alongside
other species such as chaffinches. They feed on grain and
seeds.

The demand for cut reeds for thatching has undergone something of a revival in recent decades.

At the forefront in the supply of this, our largest grass species, is the Norfolk Broads region. Reeds are usually cut every other year in suitable sites, generally during the winter months. Reed thatch is generally held to be more durable and longer lasting than the straw equivalent. However, its properties vary from site to site even within the Broads: reeds growing in brackish water are thought to be the best, for example. It has been suggested that pollution of the water by residues of agricultural fertilisers can lead to a deterioration in reed quality and an increased susceptibility to rot.

74 **Reed Bunting** *Emberiza schoeniclus* (L. 15.5cm)
Reed buntings are a common sight around the marshes and reedbeds of the Norfolk Broads. In the spring, males can be recognised by their striking black head which shows a white moustachial stripe; the male's upperparts are brown while the underparts are white. In the winter, the male has much less black on the head. The female has a more uniform brown plumage and is similar throughout the year. Reed buntings often sing their short, grating song from a bush or tall reed stem within their territory and are then easy to spot.

75 **Snow Bunting** *Plectrophenax nivalis* (L. 16cm)
Small flocks of snow buntings are regular visitors to coastal districts adjacent to the Norfolk Broads: they arrive in October and generally stay until March. During the winter months the plumage of both sexes is rather variable, containing elements of buff, white and black. Always conspicuous, however, are the large patches of white on the wings, best seen when the flock takes to the wing. Snow buntings feed mainly on seeds in the winter. They sometimes occur near the shoreline but are often encountered among dunes and marram grass.

76

77

MAMMALS

76 **Pipistrelle Bat** *Pipistrellus pipistrellus*
Several species of bats occur regularly in the Norfolk Broads region but the pipistrelle is the smallest and most regularly encountered of these. On mild evenings from early spring onwards they take to the wing at dusk, flying up and down woodland rides and over hedgerows and scrub in search of insects. Some of the larger broadland bat species, such as Daubenton's, habitually feed over water and the pipistrelle will also feed in this manner on occasions. During the winter months, pipistrelles roost in the roofs of buildings and churches.

77 **Water Vole** *Arvicola terrestris*
The water vole must surely be among the most endearing of the Norfolk Broads' mammals. Sit quietly beside a ditch or channel and you may be lucky enough to see one swim by or stop to feed on the leaves or shoots of waterside plants. They can be remarkably confiding animals, partly due to their poor eyesight. However, they also gain some degree of confidence from their excellent swimming abilities: at the first sign of danger they immediately dive and can swim underwater for quite a long distance. Water voles burrow into the waterside banks, the burrow entrance often being submerged for protection.

78 **Harvest Mouse** *Micromys minutus*
Grassy marshland meadows, patches of rank vegetation and, to a lesser degree, cornfields, are all home to the diminutive harvest mouse. The ball-shaped nests of this, our smallest rodent, are more often seen than the animal itself. Constructed from woven grass stems, the nests are suspended well away from the ground, among the grasses and thistles themselves. The mice eat seeds and will

construct nests not only during the breeding season but in winter as well. Unfortunately harvest mice have been adversely affected by increasing mechanisation in farming.

79 **Otter** *Lutra lutra*
Little is known for certain about the precise status of the otter in the Norfolk Broads, other than the fact that it is present in the area and its numbers have declined markedly over recent decades. These animals are very shy and secretive and consequently difficult to census with any degree of accuracy. Quiet visitors may be lucky enough to see one swimming or on a bank but signs of their presence are easier to spot: look for footprints in the mud or droppings — called 'spraints' — deposited on banks or waterside stones. Otters are perfectly at home in the water and feed on fish, frogs and water birds.

80 **Mole** *Talpa europaea*
Best known for the conspicuous mole-hills thrown up as it burrows, the mole is a common resident of drained land in the Norfolk Broads region. It cannot tolerate persistent flooding and so does not occur in really waterlogged terrain. Although disliked by landowners who keep animals because of their burrowing activities, the mole is a thoroughly beneficial animal when it comes to aerating the soil. Its diet comprises almost exclusively earthworms which are captured as the animal patrols its extensive burrow network.

79

80

78

81 Grey Seal *Halichoerus grypus*

Increasingly in recent years, grey seals are seen during late autumn and early winter around the Norfolk coast. Some of these individuals are females that come ashore to give birth to their pups and a few shingle and sandy beaches play regular host to these large marine mammals. Grey seals are much larger than their common relatives which also occur in the region. They have grey, rather spotted coats and males in particular have pronounced 'roman' noses and a distinctive head shape. If you are fortunate enough to see a hauled-out seal, admire it from a distance but please do not go too close.

82 Common Seal *Phoca vitulina*

As its name suggests, around the coast of East Anglia the common seal is much more numerous than its relative the grey seal. Large numbers breed and haul out along the north Norfolk coast, especially at Blakeney Point, and they are quite often sighted around the coastline adjacent to the Norfolk Broads. Common seals are relatively small animals compared to the grey seal and have rather dog-like heads. They sometimes haul out on sandy and shingle beaches and, like their relatives, should not be disturbed or harassed in any way.

83 Brown Hare *Lepus capensis*
The brown hare is a declining species both in the Norfolk Broads region and also throughout its British range. It is distinguished from the more widespread rabbit by its larger size and longer, black-tipped ears. The brown hare is a comparatively solitary animal, usually only seen in the company of others in the spring, when males fight with one another in open fields. For much of the day, hares lie crouched in a field and are most active at dawn and dusk. Regrettably, they are still persecuted in many districts by hunting.

84 Pygmy Shrew *Sorex minutus*
The tiny pygmy shrew is a common inhabitant of drier areas of land in the Norfolk Broads region. Highly active throughout the year, this tiny creature hunts almost constantly for insects, snails and other invertebrates. It feeds mainly on the ground, hunting in hedgerows and among low vegetation.

Consequently, it is seen less frequently than its high-pitched squealing is heard. Two other shrew species also occur in the region: the common shrew is similar to the pygmy shrew and lives in similar habitats; the water shrew is larger, with a black-and-white coat, and feeds mainly in shallow water.

85 Short-tailed Vole *Microtus agrestis*
Particularly during the winter months, grassland 'runs' — shallow tunnels in the short turf — can be seen in many areas of grassland in the Norfolk Broads region. These small rodents are often extremely common and form the basis of many food chains. They are eaten by almost all predators, including kestrels, owls, weasels and foxes. One of the best ways of seeing a short-tailed vole is to find a piece of corrugated iron or something similar that has been lying flat in an area of grassland. Turn this over and you are sure to find vole runs. If you are quick, and quiet enough, you will also see the voles themselves.

86 Common Frog *Rana temporaria*

As early as late February or early March, frogs begin to congregate in ponds and ditches in the Norfolk Broads. The annual ritual of mating begins in earnest and soon the waters become almost choked with masses of spawn. In order to secure themselves in a suitable position for fertilisation, pairs of frogs become locked in an embrace known as 'amplexus' where the male embraces the female with his front legs. After a week or so, tadpoles emerge from the spawn and swim throughout the water. Far more tadpoles are produced than ever become full-grown frogs. However, despite their apparent abundance at this stage, frogs have declined in recent decades, partly due to drainage and partly due to pollution.

87 Common Toad *Bufo bufo*

Like the common frog, the common toad has also declined in the Norfolk Broads in recent years. Every spring, however, good numbers still return to breed in dikes and other waterways in the region. Common toads all tend to arrive at a suitable waterbody at roughly the same time. Their calls can sometimes be heard from quite a distance and large masses of toads can be seen cavorting through the water; these masses involve a lone female toad being pursued by up to a dozen males. Toad spawn is easy to tell from frog spawn, being produced in long chains rather than large masses.

88 Natterjack Toad *Bufo calamita*

Although their population and distribution have declined markedly in recent decades, East Anglia is still one of the last strongholds of the natterjack toad. This engaging little amphibian is superficially similar to the common toad but can be told by the pale yellow stripe down its back and its habit of running rather than hopping away from danger. Natterjacks still breed in the Norfolk Broads region, mostly in marshes within extensive dune systems. During the day they remain hidden and venture out only after dark. The male's chirping song can sometimes be heard on warm evenings in May and June.

89 Grass Snake *Natrix natrix*

The grass snake is very much a creature associated with water and is an accomplished swimmer. Its diet comprises small fish and amphibians and it is perfectly happy spending much of its life in water. The grass snake is not venomous but instead holds its prey using an array of sharp, back-pointing teeth. It can be recognised by its uniform coloration and the yellow 'collar' patches on the neck. Mounds of decomposing vegetation on banks beside the water are used as incubators for their eggs. The young grass snakes usually emerge in late summer.

RIVERCRAFT

Nowadays, a great variety of boats can be seen on the Norfolk Broads.

Yachts and cruisers predominate among visitors to the region but more traditional craft can still be seen, and are often still used for the purpose they were built. Punts are long, narrow boats that are shallow in the water and double-ended, designed to be propelled with equal ease in both directions; they are used by reed cutters to negotiate narrow channels. Reed lighters are broad, flat-bottomed boats, designed for carrying considerable reed loads.

90 Four-spot Chaser *Libellula quadrimaculata*

When seen at close range, this is a distinctive dragonfly and one of the easiest species to identify. The body is rather tapering and orange-brown in colour and the four wings each bear a conspicuous dark spot, hence the common name for this insect. The four-spot chaser should be looked for from early June onwards. It is very active on sunny days, but when skies are overcast it can often be found sitting motionless on waterside vegetation. The nymphal stage of this dragonfly lives in the mud at the bottom of ditches and waterways.

91 Norfolk Aeshna *Aeshna isosceles*

The Norfolk aeshna is a speciality insect of the Norfolk Broads. Its range in Britain is entirely restricted to this region although its population has declined in recent years, probably due to pollution of the Broads. The adult insect is on the wing from about the middle of June and can usually be seen at Hickling Broad. It has clear wings, greenish eyes, a brown body and a conspicuous yellowish triangle just below the wings on the second segment of the abdomen. Areas where water-soldier flourishes usually hold good populations of the Norfolk aeshna.

92 Southern Hawker *Aeshna cyanea*

The impressive southern hawker dragonfly is widespread in the Norfolk Broads. It has clear wings and a thorax and abdomen boldly marked with blue and black on each segment. From July onwards, the southern hawker appears on the wing. At first individuals may wander away from the water and feed along hedgerows and woodland rides; by the middle of August, most have returned to the dikes and Broads from which they emerged. On sunny days, they fly vigorously over the water, catching smaller insects in flight. Their aquatic nymphal stages are equally predatory.

93 Common Darter *Sympetrum striolatum*

From July onwards, the common darter is one of the most widespread and numerous of the broadland dragonflies. It will attempt to breed in almost any type of waterbody and often in quite temporary pools. The comparatively small size and red body help identify this species which has proportionately large eyes. Common darters also persist later in the season than most other species. It is not uncommon to see a few on mild days in early November; the first severe frosts soon finish them off, however. The longer they survive in autumn, the more inclined they are, it seems, to bask in warm sunshine.

94 Large Red Damselfly

Pyrrhosoma nymphula

At first glance, this species may be thought to resemble the common darter dragonfly since both share the red coloration of their bodies. Like all other damselflies, however, the large red has fore and hindwings that are roughly identical and, at rest, these are held folded over the body and not out flat as in dragonflies. This species appears during May and June and can be seen flying slowly over the marginal vegetation beside the water. It catches small insects, such as midges, on the wing; its aquatic nymph has three flattened gills at the tail end, each bearing a dark band.

95

95 Banded Demoiselle *Calopteryx splendens*
As its scientific name suggests, this is a wonderfully colourful damselfly. The body of the male has a deep blue-green, metallic sheen and the wings bear a thumb-print-like patch of the same colour. In suitable habitats, groups of a dozen or more males sometimes gather together, flying low over the water. Females have metallic bodies but uniformly opaque, bronzy wings with a sheen. The banded demoiselle is found beside slow-flowing waters in the Norfolk Broads. Like other damselflies, the nymphal stage is aquatic and lives buried in the silt on the bottom.

96 Common Blue Damselfly *Enallagma cyathigerum*
In the Norfolk Broads region as elsewhere in most of the southern counties of England, this species is probably the most widespread and numerous of the blue damselflies. It has quite an extended flying period and is seen on the wing from June until late August in most years. Careful scrutiny of the precise shapes of the blue and black markings may be needed to distinguish it for certain from several other, less frequent, relatives in the area. Mating pairs of common blue damselflies are sometimes seen flying around in tandem, the male clasping the female with the end of his abdomen.

96

97 **Swallowtail** *Papilio machaon britannicus*
If any insect deserved to be a symbol of the Norfolk Broads
then this is it. This part of England is the only place where
swallowtail butterflies survive today and they are still a
common sight where broadland vegetation still thrives, as at
Hickling Broad. Swallowtails can hardly be mistaken for any
other butterfly. They have largely yellow wings showing a
network of black veins, and a blue and red spot on the
hindwing close to the tail streamer. When they emerge in May
and June, they often visit flowers such as ragged robin to
feed. The caterpillars feed on milk parsley and often pupate
on the stems. Sometimes a second brood emerges in the
summer.

97

98

98 **Green-veined White** *Pieris napi*
From a distance and in flight, this butterfly may look uniformly
white. Get a close view, however, particularly of the
underwing, and you will see a subtly beautiful array of greyish-
green veins which are seen to best effect when the insect is
backlit by bright sunlight. Green-veined whites are found in the
damp meadows of the Norfolk Broads where the caterpillars
feed on the leaves and shoots of cuckooflower, a common
plant of this habitat. The butterflies are seen on the wing in
April and May, and again in June and July when a second
brood emerges.

WINDMILLS

*Windmills are a feature of
the Norfolk landscape, including
that of the Norfolk Broads,
and were built originally to assist
with land drainage.*

The wind-driven sails would have
turned a water-lifting wheel, removing
water from a low-lying drainage pond.
Today, most windmills remain simply
for show, but are nevertheless an integral
part of broadland scenery.

99 **Meadow Brown** *Maniola jurtina*

Few butterfly names can be more descriptive than this one: it is indeed mostly brown and it occurs in meadows. Although they do not have especially powerful flight, meadow browns are seemingly constantly active. Once in a while, however, they pause to feed on a flower and then the upperwing can be seen well: in the female there is a broad, orange band in which an eyespot is sited while in the male the eyespot only has a small orange surround. The underwings of both sexes are a mixture of brown, yellow and orange, with a dark eyespot showing on the forewing. Meadow brown caterpillars feed on grasses.

100 **Small Tortoiseshell** *Aglais urticae*

Because it overwinters, the small tortoiseshell is often one of the first butterflies to be seen in the spring. It is often on the wing in March and successive broods mean that it may still be around as summer changes to autumn. Small tortoiseshells are frequently seen visiting flowers, whether these are thistles in a meadow or buddleia in a garden. They are also sun-lovers and are fond of basking on bare ground for minutes on end. The upperwings are brightly coloured and a mixture of reddish-orange, black and blue; the underwings, by contrast, are sombre tan and sooty-black. The caterpillars feed on nettles.

101 **Peacock** *Inachis io*

The peacock butterfly is first seen in the year in March and April, having spent the winter months hibernating in a hollow tree or an outbuilding. Like its relative, the small tortoiseshell, its caterpillars, which are black and spiky, also feed on stinging nettle. The cycle is complete after the caterpillar pupates and emerges in July as a fresh adult. Peacocks are common visitors to gardens in the region. They are also very fond of thistles and other wayside flowers and are a common sight along hedgerows. The nectar provides enough food to see the adult through the winter hibernation.

102 **Small Pearl-bordered Fritillary**
Clossiana selene

This delightful butterfly has rich orange-brown upperwings with numerous black markings. Underneath, the hindwing is a complex pattern of white, orange and brown segments. The small pearl-bordered fritillary is an insect of damp woodland rides and margins, especially where bog violet or dog violet, foodplants of the caterpillar, flourish. June is the month to look out for this butterfly. They are very active in sunshine but remain hidden among vegetation during dull weather.

103 Large Skipper

Ochlodes venata
Skipper butterflies, and this species in particular, can sometimes look surprisingly moth-like while resting with their wings half spread. Large skippers have brown upperwings, those of the male looking more orange than those of the female. The underwing in both sexes is buffish-brown. Like other species of skippers, the caterpillars of the large skipper feed on grasses. Not surprisingly, therefore, the adult is a common meadow butterfly, visiting flowers in this habitat and in hedgerows for nectar. Large skippers are seen on the wing during June and July.

103

104

104 **Alder** *Alnus glutinosa*
Alder is a typical tree of marshy, waterlogged habitats,
having nitrogen-fixing root nodules to aid its nutrient
supply. In many areas, it can form large stands of
woodland and these are known as alder 'carrs'. When full
grown, it can reach a height of 20m and has rather
fissured bark. The leaves are oval but with a blunt, almost
cut-off tip; they are dark green and shiny on the upper
surface. The cones, which persist, often attract small
parties of siskins and redpolls which feed on the seeds.
When cut, alder wood soon turns bright orange.

105 **Guelder-rose** *Viburnum opulus*
Sometimes seen growing in similar situations to alder,
guelder-rose eventually forms small trees up to 3.5
metres high. In early summer, circular heads of white
flowers are produced and these are visited by pollinating
insects. In the autumn, these give rise to clusters of juicy,
red berries; not surprisingly, these are popular with
migrant thrushes and other birds that arrive at this
season. Guelder-rose has opposite leaves which are three
to five-lobed, the lobes themselves being toothed.

105

106 Privet *Ligustrum vulgare*

Privet is a common shrub in many of the mature areas of alder carr woodland and scrub in the Norfolk Broads region. It is at least partly evergreen and bushes may reach a height of 4m or more. The leaves of privet are oval, pointed and shiny above but rather matt beneath. The individual flowers are small and white, carried in dense, conical sprays; the flowers have a heavy, almost musk-like scent and are seen in the late spring. Privet berries are black and shiny when ripe, but poisonous. The plant is also used for garden hedging.

107 Hawthorn *Crataegus monogyna*

Hawthorn is a common hedgerow shrub throughout the region. It can grow to a height of 10m but is usually considerably smaller than this. Hawthorn is a deciduous plant, the deeply lobed leaves appearing in the springtime. The flowers are seen in May and June, hence its alternative name of May blossom. They are 8-12mm across, white, and carried in flat-topped clusters; synchronised flowering can mean that whole bushes turn white. In the autumn, sprays of red berries appear and provide a feast for migrant and winter birds alike.

106

107

THE LARGE COPPER

Although the region's most showy butterfly, the swallowtail, still survives in good numbers in the Norfolk Broads, another attractive species is no longer found.

The beautiful large copper became extinct in Britain more than a century ago. It is not known for certain why it disappeared because its foodplant, great water dock, still grows here; changes in land management and water level may have had something to do with it. If you want to see large coppers nowadays, you will have to visit English Nature's reserve at Woodwalton Fen where a colony of the Dutch subspecies has been established.

Top: Large Copper larva
Bottom: Large Copper Lycaena dispar batavus

108 Hop *Humulus lupulus*
Sprawling along hedgerows, up telegraph poles and in scrub and alder carr, the hop is a common sight in the Norfolk Broads region. It is a climbing and trailing perennial plant whose square stems twist in a clockwise manner and carry palmate, stalked leaves. Male and female flowers are produced on separate plants; the female ones are cone-like catkins and these are the familiar hops used for brewing beer. Although in many parts of Britain the hop is naturalised from cultivation, in this area it is probably native.

109 Redshank *Polygonum persicaria*
A relative of bistort, redshank is an often abundant weed of waste ground, cultivated land and disturbed soil. It is, however, often overlooked because of its rather drab appearance. The plant thrives particularly well in damp situations and is consequently often found on the muddy banks of broadland waterways. Redshank is a sprawling plant with lanceolate leaves that bear a dark blotch near the centre. The stems are usually slightly reddish and the pink flowers are carried in dense spikes which are either terminal or arise from leaf axils.

110 Ragged Robin *Lychnis flos-cuculi*
It would be rather difficult to mistake ragged robin for any other plant when it is in flower. The pink flowers comprise petals that are each divided into four, ragged lobes; several are carried together in a loose head. The leaves are narrow and lanceolate and can easily be overlooked if the flowers are absent. Ragged robin is a plant of wet meadows and fens, thriving in permanently damp soils; not surprisingly, it is often common in the Norfolk Broads. The attractive flowers are produced from May to July.

111 Yellow Water-lily *Nuphar lutea*
Although white water-lily does occur in the Norfolk Broads region, its yellow cousin is more widespread and generally more common. The yellow water-lily has large, rounded, floating leaves that can be 35cm in diameter; they are covered in numerous parallel veins. From June to September, fairly tall stalks are carried above the water and bear the yellow flowers that are 5cm in diameter. After the flowers have been fertilised, the stalks gradually droop towards the water. In some broadland situations, yellow water-lily almost carpets the surface of the water.

112 Marsh-marigold *Caltha palustris*
Also known as kingcups, marsh-marigold is an attractive and distinctive marshland plant. The bright yellow flowers are 50mm across and buttercup-like. They are carried on long stalks and are produced from March to July. Petals are in fact absent in this species, the yellow portions of the flower being sepals. The plant is generally robust and the leaves, 10cm in diameter, are kidney-shaped. Marsh-marigold grows in wetland sites locally throughout the Norfolk Broads region. It can be found in damp woodland, meadows and even in shallow water.

113 Greater Spearwort *Ranunculus lingua*
Flowering at any time between June and September, greater spearwort is one of the most attractive and showy members of the buttercup family. The bright yellow flowers comprise five petals and may measure 45mm in diameter. Greater spearwort is invariably associated with watery habitats and pond margins, fens and marshy hollows all provide the right conditions for the plant. In the Norfolk Broads, as elsewhere in Britain, it is a rather local plant and has been much affected by problems affecting the aquatic environment in general, namely pollution, agricultural run-off and alteration of the water table.

114 Lesser Celandine *Ranunculus ficaria*
Hedgerows, woodlands and bare, damp ground provide ideal habitats for lesser celandine. The attractive, buttercup-like flowers appear as early as February but most flowering occurs in April and May. The flowers themselves are bright yellow, roughly 25mm across and comprise eight to 12 petals and three sepals. They arise on fairly long stalks from clusters of dark green heart-shaped leaves that are rather fleshy. In some parts of the Norfolk Broads, lesser celandine forms large patches or even carpets areas of woodland floor.

108

109

115

116

115 **Cuckooflower** *Cardamine pratensis*
Also known as lady's smock, this attractive flower is a
member of the crucifer flower, the name deriving from the
flower pattern of the family, namely four petals arranged in
the shape of a cross. Cuckooflower is a plant of damp
meadows and similar grassy habitats; it thrives in wet
meadows in the Norfolk Broads region but not in the reedbeds
themselves. The plant has a basal rosette of pinnate leaves
from which arises a tall stem bearing a few leaves.
The pale lilac flowers are 15mm across and are carried in
terminal clusters; they appear from April to June.

116 **Grass-of-Parnassus** *Parnassus palustris*
In the Norfolk Broads region, grass-of-Parnassus is a plant of
fens and marshes. It thrives best in areas where it does not
suffer competition from taller, more vigorous plants; the
practice of cutting fen vegetation, more favoured in the past
than at present, actually favoured this species. Grass-of-
Parnassus has heart-shaped leaves; those at the base have
stalks while the stem leaves are stalkless and clasping.
The attractive, cup-shaped flowers appear from June to
September. They are white and comprise five petals which
are beautifully lined with green veins.

117 **Meadowsweet** *Filipendula vulgaris*
Riverside, broadland margins and marshy meadows are home
to the attractive meadowsweet which sometimes thrives and
grows in large, showy patches. The individual flowers are
quite small but they are produced in dense clusters forming
terminal inflorescences. These are carried on tall stems which
may be more than 1m tall and the sight of hundreds of flower
heads growing side by side is an impressive one; from June
to September is the time to look for them. The leaves of
meadowsweet are compound and comprise both toothed and
lobed leaflets.

118 **Dog-rose** *Rosa canina*
The attractive dog-rose is a common sight in the Norfolk
Broads region, growing in hedgerows, scrub and on banks,
usually on soil that is seldom inundated. The attractive, pink
flowers appear during June and July and are carried on
stalks. They are 40-50mm in diameter and, like other wild
roses, have petals and sepals in fives. The plant has hairless
leaflets and trailing or arching stems bearing robust, curved
prickles. In the autumn, the fruits mature to become the
familiar red rosehips which provide a feast for small mammals
and birds.

119 **Marsh Cinquefoil** *Potentilla palustris*
Marsh cinquefoil is a distinctive but unusual-looking flower that is locally fairly common in the Norfolk Broads region. It grows in fens and marshy habitats, often where the soil is waterlogged. The flowers comprise five pointed maroon-coloured petals which superficially resemble the plant's five purple sepals. The numbers of flowering parts betray this plant's membership of the rose family. Marsh cinquefoil grows to a height of about 40cm and has leaves which are pinnate or trifoliate, and has leaflets with toothed margins. The flowers appear from May to July.

120 **Silverweed** *Potentilla anserina*
Silverweed is widespread and common throughout Britain and especially so in the Norfolk Broads region. Because of its habit of sprawling across tracks and paths, it is often overlooked, but it is nevertheless an attractive plant when studied closely. Silverweed is so-called because the underside, and sometimes both sides, of the pinnate, toothed leaves are silvery in appearance due to a covering of hairs. The flowers are bright yellow and are up to 20mm across. Another feature of this plant is that long, red stolons are produced and give rise to new individuals; this is most noticeable on bare, muddy ground.

121 **Greater Bird's-foot-trefoil** *Lotus uliginosus*
Damp meadows, fens and marshes are home to greater bird's-foot-trefoil. Although related and similar to the common bird's-foot-trefoil of dry grassland, this plant is much taller, up to 50cm, and is inclined to sprawl and trail through the vegetation with which it grows. The name 'trefoil' refers to the leaves appearing to be trifoliate — they are, in fact, divided into five but two of the leaflets appear separate. The yellow flowers are arranged in heads of three to seven and are carried on long stalks; they appear from June to August.

122 **Tufted Vetch** *Vicia cracca*
Tufted vetch grows in grassy places of all sorts but, in the Norfolk Broads region, is often found in surprisingly wet fens and marsh, so long as the vegetation is not too rank. This attractive member of the pea family produces tall, dense heads of bluish-lilac flower which sometimes become rather bleached and washed out with age. These appear from June to August, the sprawling plants often producing large numbers of heads within a relatively small area. The plant is hairless and has pinnate leaves comprising six to 12 leaflets, at the end of which are tendrils.

123 **Marsh Mallow** *Althaea officinalis*
Tolerant of salt spray and the influence of the sea, marsh mallow is often found near to the coast or even just above the high-tide line on saltmarshes. In the Norfolk Broads, it also grows on waterside banks and in marshes inland. Marsh mallow is a rather distinctive plant which grows to 2m and is very downy-hairy. The leaves have a triangular outline, rounded at the base, and the flowers are usually around 35mm across. They are pale pink and produced both from the leaf axils and in terminal clusters. Marsh mallow is only locally common in the region.

124 **Purple-loosestrife** *Lysimachia salicaria*
During July and August, the tall spikes of purple-loosestrife are a common sight in the Norfolk Broads. The plant grows in a variety of habitats but is nowhere so obvious as along river banks and waterside margins. Purple-loosestrife grows to a height of 1m or more with flowering spikes that themselves can be 20cm long. The individual flowers are reddish-purple and comprise six petals; they are roughly 12mm across and are popular with pollinating insects. The leaves are oval to lanceolate in outline and are carried in opposite pairs or groups of three.

125 **Great Willowherb** *Epilobium hirsutum*
Codlins-and-cream is another name for this large, showy plant. Great willowherb can reach a height of 2m and often grows in large stands along the banks of waterways or in wet corners of marshes and fens. Attractive, four-petalled flowers are produced during July and August. They are roughly 25mm across and pink, but with white floral parts in the centre. They are produced in a loose inflorescence and carried on stalks. Study the plants closely and you may find the extraordinary caterpillars of the elephant hawk moth, which have large eyespots.

126 **Rosebay Willowherb** *Epilobium angustifolium*
Stands of the conspicuous and showy rosebay willowherb are a familiar sight in the Norfolk Broads region. The plant grows on waste ground, cleared areas and beside tracks and paths. It also grows on areas that have been recently burnt, hence its alternative name of 'fireweed'. Rosebay willowherb can reach a height of 2m but is usually shorter. The leaves are lanceolate and arranged in a spiral manner up the stem. At the top, a loose, conical spray of flowers is produced; individual flowers have four petals and are pinkish-purple. After flowering, seeds, with parachutes of hairs, are carried on the wind.

124

125

126

FISH

The Norfolk Broads region is home to more than half the species of freshwater fish that occur in Britain as a whole: upwards of 25 species are regularly seen or caught.

These include all the more familiar British fish, such as rudd, roach, common bream, tench, perch and pike; many extremely large specimens of each have been recorded in the past. Unfortunately, populations of most species have declined markedly in recent years. These changes are usually attributed to pollution, mainly from boat fuel, and disturbance by watercraft in general.

Top: Rudd Scardinius erythrop thalamus
Bottom: Pike Esox lucius

five or six arranged up the stem. The small, white flowers are 3mm across and have four white petals; they appear in small clusters at the ends of stems from June to August. As the name suggests, bedstraws were once used for bedding when dried.

131 Hedge Bindweed *Calystegia sepium*
In many broadland locations, this climbing, trailing plant becomes really conspicuous by the end of the summer as it sprawls through fenland vegetation and along hedgerows; in some locations it can almost smother the plants that support

127 Wild Angelica
Angelica sylvestris
A member of the carrot family, wild angelica is a large, stout plant producing impressive umbels of flowers. Although it will grow in damp woodlands, it is mainly a plant of fens and marshes in the Norfolk Broads region, sometimes towering above the surrounding vegetation at a height of 2m or more. The hollow stem of the plant is often tinged purple and carries large leaves which are triangular and highly pinnately divided. The flowers are whitish, sometimes tinged with green or pink; they are carried in dense umbels with several umbels in each plant. The winged seeds float — a useful adaptation in a watery environment.

127

128 Water Violet *Hottonia palustris*
A truly aquatic plant, water violet is at home in quiet channels and ditches in the Norfolk Broads. The leaves are finely divided, the degree of division depending on whether they are floating or submerged. Only the flower spikes emerge from the water and, during May and June, carry terminal clusters of pale lilac flowers; these have five petals and are roughly 20mm across. In suitable habitats, water violet can form dense stands covering a considerable area. It is, however, a declining plant which is adversely affected by changes to water quality, level and disturbance.

129 Bogbean *Menyanthes trifoliata*
The aptly named bogbean grows in the wetter parts of fens and marshy meadows in the Norfolk Broads. The name derives partly from its preferred habitat and partly from the appearance and texture of the trifoliate leaves that resemble those of broad bean. Most of the plant is aquatic and it is generally only these leaves and the flower spike that are emergent. The flowers are carried in spikes up to 25cm tall. Individual flowers are pinkish-white and have five petals that are fringed with hairs; they appear from April to June and are locally common in the region.

130 Common Marsh-bedstraw *Galium palustre*
Several rather similar species of white-flowering bedstraw occur in the region, but common marsh-bedstraw is the most widespread in wet sites in fens and sedge-filled meadows. Like other bedstraws, the leaves are narrow and rather spiky; in this species they are 5-15mm long and carried in whorls of

its growth. Hedge bindweed has twisted stems and leaves which are shaped like arrow heads and often more than 100mm long. The flowers are white, trumpet-shaped and often 30mm in diameter and 40mm long. Hedge bindweed flowers from June to September and is common throughout the region.

132 Gipsywort *Lycopus europaeus*
Watery margins along the edges of broadland waterways are home to gipsywort. This member of the mint family is a branched perennial herb; the degree of branching and the plant's height are, however, variable. The leaves are oval to triangular in outline and deeply toothed. The flowers are small and pale pinkish; they are arranged in whorls towards the ends of the branching stems, and each have a pair of leaf-like, toothed bracts. Gipsywort flowers from June to September and is also found in damp alder carr woodland throughout the region.

129

132

133

131

130

133 Water Mint *Mentha aquatica*

Walk through many areas of marsh and fen in the Norfolk Broads and a strong smell of mint fills the air. This fragrance comes from the water mint that grows freely here and along the banks and margins of many of the waterways. The leaves of the plant are oval and rather shiny. The individual flowers are pinkish-lilac and 3mm long, they are carried in densely packed terminal clusters as well as in dense whorls down the stem on occasions. Water mint flowers from July to October in some years and the plant itself may reach a height of 50cm or more.

134 Devil's-bit Scabious *Succisa pratensis*

Devil's-bit scabious is a plant of fens, marshes and wet meadows and does particularly well where cutting prevents a growth of rank vegetation. Although the plant is a member of the teasel family, the flower heads are very like those of the scabiouses — members of the daisy family. They are usually 20mm across and comprise pinkish-lilac florets arranged compactly in a hemispherical head. There are spoon-shaped basal leaves and narrow stem leaves. Devil's-bit scabious is popular with pollinating insects and flowers from June onwards, and into October in some years.

134

135 **Hemp Agrimony** *Eupatorium cannabinum*
Large stands of hemp agrimony are a notable feature of damp marshes, waterside margins and fens in the Norfolk Broads region. This large, showy plant can grow to a height of more than 1.5m and produces heads of flowers, grouped together to form flattish clusters. The individual flowers are pinkish but sometimes paler or darker; the seeds are hairy and wind-borne. Hemp agrimony has stalked basal leaves and three-or five-lobed leaves on the stem. It flowers from July to September and is locally very common throughout the region.

136 **Frogbit** *Hydrocharis morsus-ranae*
As you walk beside slow-flowing waterways and dykes in the Norfolk Broads, keep an eye open for what look like miniature water-lily leaves floating on the surface of the water during the summer months. These are likely to be the leaves of the intriguingly named frogbit, a water plant that is more widespread and common here than anywhere else in England. Delicate, three-petalled white flowers are raised above the surface of the water at any time between June and August. The petals do not last long, however, before they fall and the stalk disappears beneath the water's surface.

137 Flowering Rush *Butomus umbellatus*
Search along the edges of reedy marshes and along
overgrown dykes and you may be lucky enough to find
flowering rush. This aquatic perennial produces long basal
leaves and flower stems that can be more than 1m tall. The
pale pink flowers have three petals, three sepals and are
roughly 25mm across. They are produced in a terminal umbel
often comprising 15 or more flowers. In Britain, flowering rush
is an extremely local and rather scarce plant. In the Norfolk
Broads, despite having declined in recent years, it is still fairly
common and widespread.

138 Common Water-plantain *Alisma plantago-aquatica*
As its name suggests, common water-plantain is indeed fairly
numerous in the Norfolk Broads region. It is an aquatic
perennial which thrives in the muddy margins of dykes,
ditches and broadland backwaters. The plant has robust,
rather oval-shaped leaves which are stalked, at least 15cm
long and produced from the substrate. A tall flowering stalk,
up to 1m in length, is produced and, from June to August,
carries an extremely branched inflorescence of three-petalled
flowers which are whitish and slightly tinged with pinkish-
purple.

139 Water-soldier *Stratiotes aloides*
The Norfolk Broads and surrounding wetlands are the best
places to see this plant in Britain. Water-soldier is an aquatic
perennial that remains submerged for most of the year. During
the summer months, however, the plant rises to the surface
and produces its rather insignificant, three-petalled white
flowers. The plant is sometimes so numerous that whole
waterways become almost choked with it. Water-soldier is
characterised by having rosettes of tough, spiny-edged
leaves, most of which rise at a sharp angle from the base.

140 Branched Bur-reed *Sparganium erectum*
Branched bur-reed is a common plant in the Norfolk Broads,
growing at the edge of water and in the muddy margins of
dykes and waterways. Without its flowers, it looks deceptively
similar to the reeds and sedges with which it often grows.
During the summer months, however, a tall spike, often 1m or
more high, is produced bearing a branched inflorescence of
flowers. These are carried in globular heads arranged along
each branch and appear between June to August. Unbranched
bur-reed (*S. emersum*) also occurs in the region. It is similar
but, as its name suggests, the inflorescence is unbranched.

141 Yellow Iris *Iris pseudacorus*
Also know as yellow flag, few people will fail to recognise this conspicuous and showy flower as an iris. Clumps of this distinctive plant are a common sight in marshes and fens, and along the margins of waterways in the Norfolk Broads. The leaves of yellow iris are lanceolate in outline, broad and tough; they may reach almost 1m in length on occasions. The flowers are bright yellow, up to 10cm across and carried in groups of two or three; they are very popular with pollinating insects. Brown seed capsules ripen in the autumn.

142 Early Marsh Orchid *Dactylorhiza incarnata*
Three species of closely related orchid occur in the Norfolk Broads region, belonging to genus *Dactylorhiza*. Of these, the early marsh orchid is, as its name implies, one of the first to flower, doing so from May to July. Although the plant is rather variable, it always has unspotted, lanceolate leaves and a compact and dense inflorescence of flowers. Individual flowers are usually flesh-pink with the lower lip folded back on itself. Early marsh orchid is found in fens and marshes and does best in areas where rank vegetation is prevented from dominating.

143 Southern Marsh Orchid *Dactylorhiza praetermissa*
The tall spikes of southern marsh orchid are an impressive sight during June and July. Around the Norfolk Broads region, the plant grows in low-cut fens and marshes, often in similar habitats to early marsh orchid, with which its flowering period overlaps slightly; hybrids between the two species are occasionally detected. Southern marsh orchid can grow to a height of 70cm. It has broad, lanceolate leaves which are unspotted and tall spikes of reddish-purple flowers. Individual flowers have a flattish lower lip which is shallowly three-lobed.

144 Common Spotted Orchid *Dactylorhiza fuchsii*
Although the common spotted orchid is found in similar habitats to the two related species of marsh orchid of the region, it also occurs in drier areas of grassland. As its name suggests, its has dark-spotted leaves which are broad lanceolate at the base but become narrower up the stem. The flowers spikes are usually long and the whole plant can reach a height of 60cm or more. Individual flowers are pale pink but heavily marked with deep purple spots and streaks; the lip has three more or less equal lobes. Common spotted orchid flowers from June to August.

142

141

145 Fen Orchid *Liparis loeselii*
The Norfolk Broads is one of only three regions in Britain where the rare fen orchid still survives. Compared to many of our orchids, it is not especially showy but its rarity value gets keen botanists excited. Fen orchid characteristically has two rather large, basal leaves which appear to almost form a basal cup. From the centre of this a loose spike of flowers is produced, growing to 15cm or more. The individual flowers are greenish-yellow, rather linear and recurved and quite attractive when viewed in close-up. As the name suggests, fen orchid grows in fens where competing rank vegetation is kept to a minimum by winter grazing or cutting.

146 Marsh Helleborine *Epipactis palustris*
The marsh helleborine is one of the most appealing orchids in the Norfolk Broads region, partly because of the colours and texture of the flowers, but also because it is usually seen growing in fairly large stands. It is a plant of marshes and fens and, although it grows to a height of 50cm, cannot tolerate excessive competition from more vigorous plants. The leaves are oval and pointed at the base, but become more linear up the stem. The flowers are carried in a loose spike. Individual flowers have a pale-pink, frilly-edged lip; all the petals and sepals have an almost crystalline texture.

147 Common Reedmace *Typha latifolia*
Sometimes inaccurately referred to as bulrush, common reedmace, together with its close relative, lesser reedmace, are familiar broadland plants. Common reedmace grows to a height of 2m or more and is found growing from shallow water along the margins of waterways and in dykes. The leaves are long, lanceolate and tough, and grow mostly from the base. They sometimes exceed the height of the flower which comprises a sausage-like cylinder of female flowers topped with a thin spike of male flowers. In lesser reedmace, the male and female flowers are separated by a gap.

148 **Common Reed** *Phragmites communis*

If any plant were chosen to symbolise the Norfolk Broads then it ought to be the common reed. Not only does this tall member of the grass family grow in abundance in the region, but it also underpins the economy of the area: reeds are cut on an annual basis for thatching houses. Common reed can, on occasions, grow to a height of 3m or more. It will only survive in soils that are damp or waterlogged, but can thrive when growing from several feet of water as well. The plant can even flourish if the water is partly brackish.

149 **Marsh Fern** *Thelypteris palustris*

The marsh fern has one of its strongholds in Britain in the Norfolk Broads region; it is locally common in parts of the Broads but decidedly uncommon in the rest of the country. As its name suggests, this rather delicate species fern grows in marshy conditions. However, because it requires a degree of shade in order to thrive, it is most commonly seen in alder carrs. The stalked fronds grow in clumps between clumps of tussock sedge and are best looked for in early spring before the shade of the tree canopy makes their habitat rather gloomy.

150 **Royal Fern** *Osmunda regalis*

In terms of size and stature, the royal fern is indeed a king among its kind: it is the largest fern in Britain and can grow to a height of nearly 2m in some cases. This species has declined markedly in Britain in recent years, mainly due to the effects of land drainage, but still thrives in parts of the Norfolk Broads region. The fronds are regularly branched, each branch bearing oval-lanceolate leaflets. From the centre of clumps of royal fern develop spore-bearing fronds, the spore bodies being orange-brown when mature. Royal fern grows in damp, swampy situations, mainly in alder carrs.

151 **Crested Buckler Fern** *Dryopteris cristata*

Having declined markedly in the parts of southern England where it once occurred, mainly due to land drainage, crested buckler fern now has its last British stronghold in the Norfolk Broads region. The fronds are carried on long, scaly stalks; the outer fronds in a clump are spreading while the inner ones, which carry spore bodies, are more upright. The fronds have ten or more branches, the lobes of each branch being further divided. Crested buckler fern grows in marshy places, usually among rushes, sedges and sphagnum moss.

148

In 1989, the Broads Act was passed by Parliament in an attempt to regulate potentially conflicting interests within the region, notably the needs of wildlife, tourism and the maintenance of the local way of life.

The Broads Authority was set up and the Norfolk Broads is now a national park in all but name. Within the area there are three sites designated as National Nature Reserves and these are Bure Marshes, Ludham Marshes and Hickling Broad.

Swallowtail larva Papilio machaon sub britannicus

PLACES OF INTEREST

The following places to visit lie within the Norfolk Broads area and can be located on the map on pages 4 and 5.

• Beeston Hall
Beeston St Lawrence.
Tel: 01692 630771.
Georgian country house. Woodland walks in the surrounding grounds. *Open Easter to mid-September on certain days.*

• Berney Arms Windmill
There is no suitable vehicular access to this seven-storey high windmill, now in the care of English Heritage. Houses an exhibition about windmills. *Open Easter to September daily.*

• Burgh Castle
Burgh Castle.
Tel: 01493 700605.
Ruins of a castle built by the Romans as part of their coastal defence. English Heritage. *Open at any reasonable time.*

• Caister Castle Motor Museum
Caister-on-Sea.
Tel: 0157284 251.
A display of vehicles from the late 19th century on. Also a moated castle and tower. *Open mid-May to September daily, except Saturday.*

• Fritton Lake Country Park
Fritton.
Lakes, woodland walks, picnic areas and adventure playground. *Open April to October daily.*

• Pettitts Crafts
Reedham.
Tel: 01493 70094.
Peacocks, pheasants, ornamental birds and birds of prey in an aviary. Also waterfowl. Picnic area, feathercraft workshop, adventure playground, miniature railway and cafe.

• Thrigby Hall Wildlife Gardens
Filby. Tel: 01493 369477.
Mammmals, birds and reptiles in landscaped gardens. Tropical house, deer paddocks and lake. *Open all year daily.*

USEFUL ADDRESSES

Broads Authority
Thomas Harvey House, 18 Colegate, Norwich

Countryside Commission
John Dower House
Crescent Place, Cheltenham, Glos GL50 3RA

English Nature (Headquarters)
Northminster House, Peterborough PE1 1VA

National Trust (Regional Office)
Blickling, Norwich NR11 6NF

Norfolk County Council
County Hall, Norwich NR1 2DH

Norfolk Naturalists' Trust
72 Cathedral Close, Norwich NR1 4DF

RSPB (Headquarters)
The Lodge, Sandy, Beds SG19 2DL

Wildfowl Trust
Slimbridge, Glos GL2 7BT

INDEX